Just for that you've got the mumps!

Oysters and ice cream, pickles and cake!
Now you have a belly ache!

Quakes and shakes and wails and wiggles!
Turn around, you've got the giggles!

Ha ha! Haw haw! Hee hee hee!
Athlete's foot I give to thee!

Up your back
and down your britches,
scratch, my dear,
you've got the itches.

Ratstail hangnail!
Gadzooks-zounds!
You weigh
sixteen hundred pounds!

Hocus pocus!
Ginger beer!
It's time for you
to disappear.

Wiggledy wiggledy,
let's end the game.
It's time for you
to do the same.

Though each of them
was out of sight,
they cast their spells
all through the night.

They turned roses into vaseline
and spring rain into gasoline
and spider webs to wire
and forests into fire
and apples into plastic
and elephants, elastic
and then they grew more drastic.

A radiator alligator elevator rose,
and a purple goat
sank in a boat
when her toes
became her nose.

And in the early
morning light
the witch and wizard
looked a sight.

Their creezles and beezles
and razzle and dazzle
had worn them each down
to a raggedy frazzle.

"Though spells that are vicious
are truly delicious,
it takes too much out
of us both."

"The results are unsightly,"
said the wizard politely.
"And what's more it might
stunt our growth."

So ended
the fighting and fuming,
so ended
the witcherly wizardly
booming,
the allacazamming
and allacazooming.

They cared no longer
to see who was stronger,
for what is a curse
more or less?

What with lizards and toads
all over the roads,
it will take them forever
to clean up the mess.

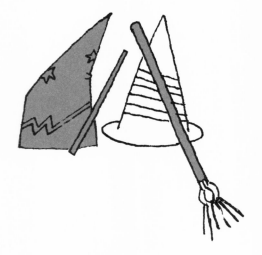

92 93 97

NO RENEWALS!

PLEASE RETURN BOOK AND REQUEST
AGAIN.